MY FIRST FIVE YEARS

A New Millennium

The Year 2000

2000

- CONTENTS -

- CONTENTS -

- MY BIRTH -

My name is
_____

_____

I was born on
_____

at
_____

_____

_____

_____

The time was
_____

_____

I was delivered by
_____

_____

_____

_____

I weighed
_____

and measured
_____

My eyes were
_____

My hair was
_____

- MEMENTOS -

My hospital tag

A lock of hair

My Birth Announcement

- NEWSPAPER CLIPPINGS -

- SPECIAL MESSAGES -

Mother

_____

_____

_____

_____

Father

_____

_____

_____

_____

Family

_____

_____

_____

_____

Friends

_____

_____

_____

_____

- VISITORS AND GIFTS -

_____

_____

_____

_____

_____

_____

_____

_____

- SIGNS -

_____

Star Sign

Chinese Year

Birthstone

Birth Flower

Birth Day Horoscope

_____

_____

_____

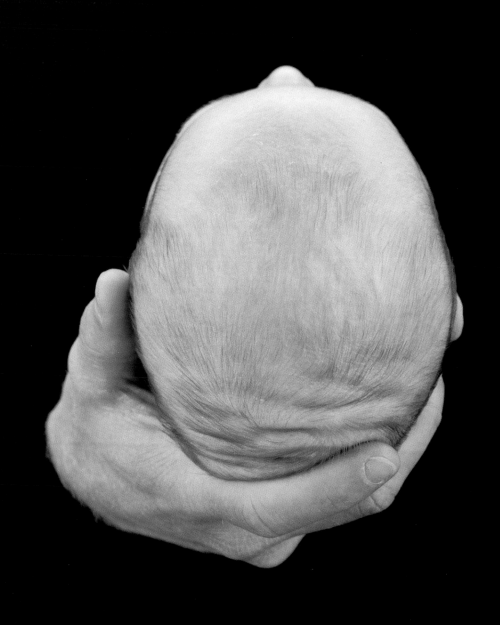

- NAMING -

My full name is _____

My name was chosen by _____

_____

_____

because _____

_____

_____

My pet names are _____

_____

_____

Ceremonies celebrating my birth _____

at _____

_____

_____

Comments _____

_____

_____

_____

_____

- MY FAMILY TREE -

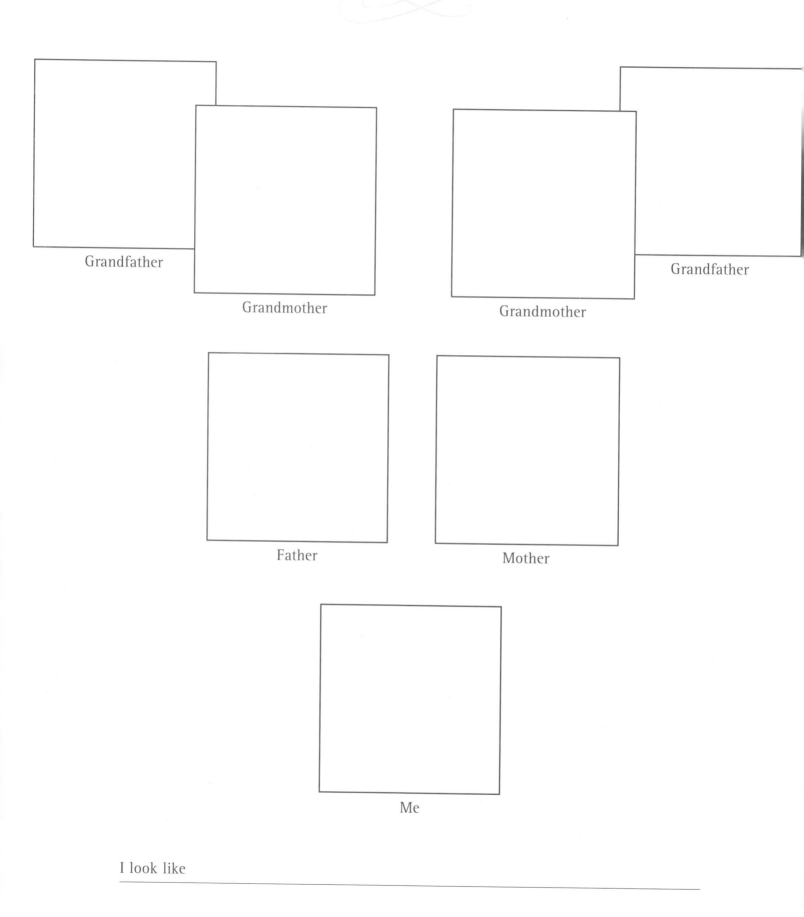

Grandfather

Grandmother

Grandmother

Grandfather

Father

Mother

Me

I look like

- PHOTOGRAPHS -

- THREE MONTHS -

Weight

Length

Comments

- SIX MONTHS -

Weight

Length

Comments

- NINE MONTHS -

Weight

Length

Comments

- MY FIRST BIRTHDAY -

I live at

My height is

Weight

Sayings

Toys

Pets

Books

- MY PARTY -

Date

Where held

Friends and relations there

My presents

- MILESTONES -

I first smiled

laughed

grasped a toy

I slept through the night

I held my head up

rolled over

sat up

I first crawled

stood up

walked

My first tooth

My first word

Other milestones

- FOOD -

My first solid food

I was weaned

I drank from a cup

I fed myself

Finger food

I like

I don't like

- MY FIRST CHRISTMAS -

It was at
_____

Other people there
_____

My presents
_____

- MY FIRST VACATION -

It was at

Date

The weather was

Other people there

What we did

Comments

- CLOTHES -

The first time I dressed myself

I wore

My favorite dress-ups

I won't wear

Comments

- FAVORITES -

Music

_____

Rhymes

_____

_____

_____

Clothes

_____

_____

Animals

_____

_____

Activities

_____

_____

Television programs

_____

I really don't like

_____

_____

- BEST FRIENDS -

Comments

One Year

Two Years

Three Years

Four Years

Comments

Five Years

- MY SECOND BIRTHDAY -

I live at

_____

_____

_____

My height is

Weight

Sayings

_____

Toys

_____

_____

Pets

_____

_____

Books

_____

_____

_____

_____

_____

- PHOTOGRAPHS -

- MY PARTY -

Date

Where held

Friends and relations there

My presents

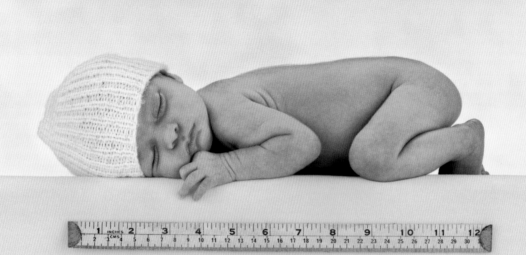

- MY THIRD BIRTHDAY -

I live at

My height is

Weight

Sayings

Toys

Pets

Books

- MY PARTY -

Date

Where held

Friends and relations there

My presents

- MY FOURTH BIRTHDAY -

I live at

My height is

Weight

Sayings

Toys

Pets

Books

- PRE-SCHOOL -

I started on

My pre-school is called *Lost Mountain Baptist Pre School*

My friends there are *Ryan*

What I like to do there

- MY PARTY -

Date

Where held

Friends and relations there

My presents

- MY FIFTH BIRTHDAY -

I live at

My height is

Weight

Sayings

Toys

Pets

Books

- MY PARTY -

Date ·

Where held

Friends and relations there

My presents

- KINDERGARTEN -

My first day at kindergarten was on

The kindergarten is called

My teacher is

What I did on the first day

My friends are

Comments

- WRITING -

I could recite the alphabet

I started to write

I began to read

My writing

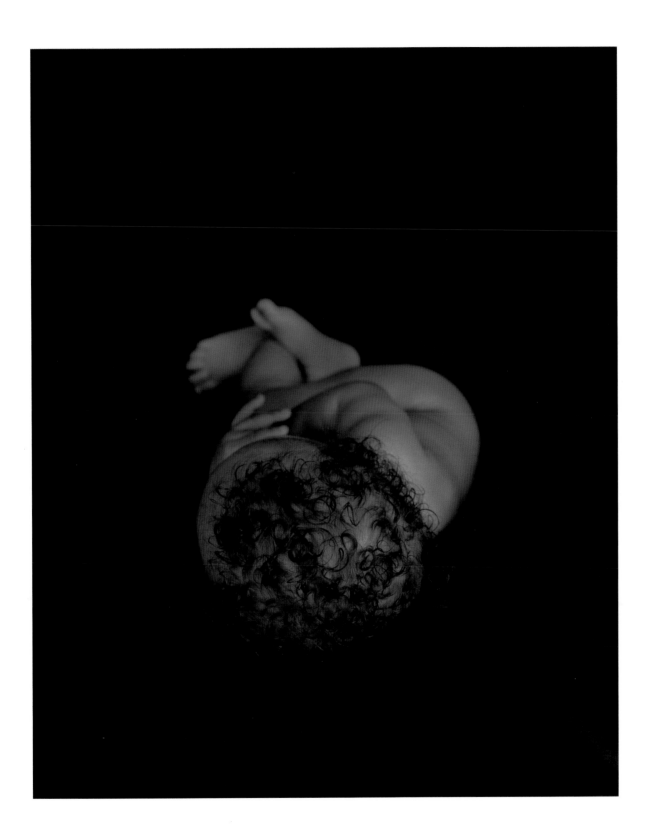

- HEALTH -

IMMUNIZATION

Age	Vaccine	Date given

Illnesses

Allergies

Comments

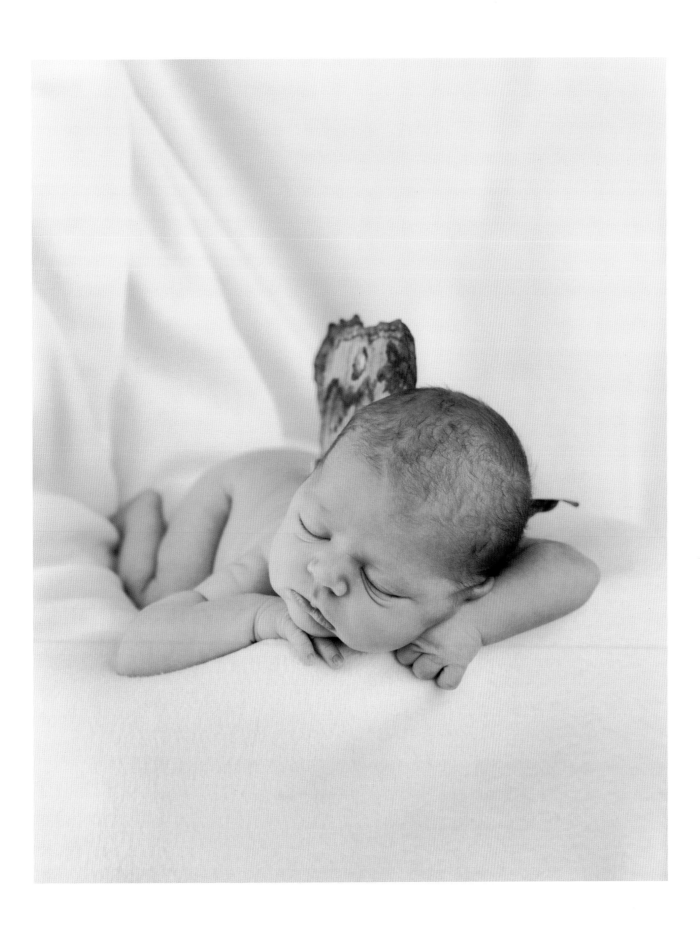

- MY HEIGHT -

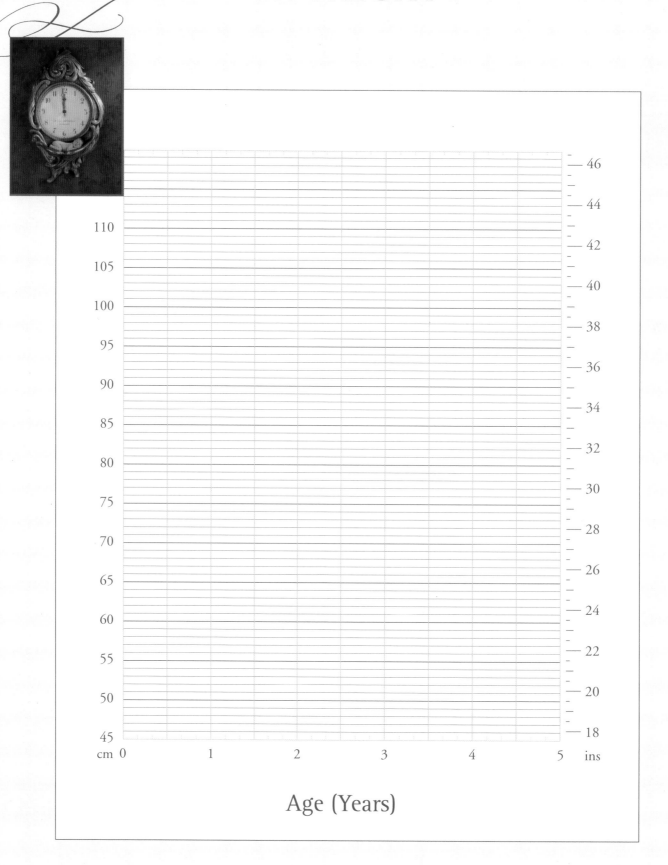

Age (Years)

- MY WEIGHT -

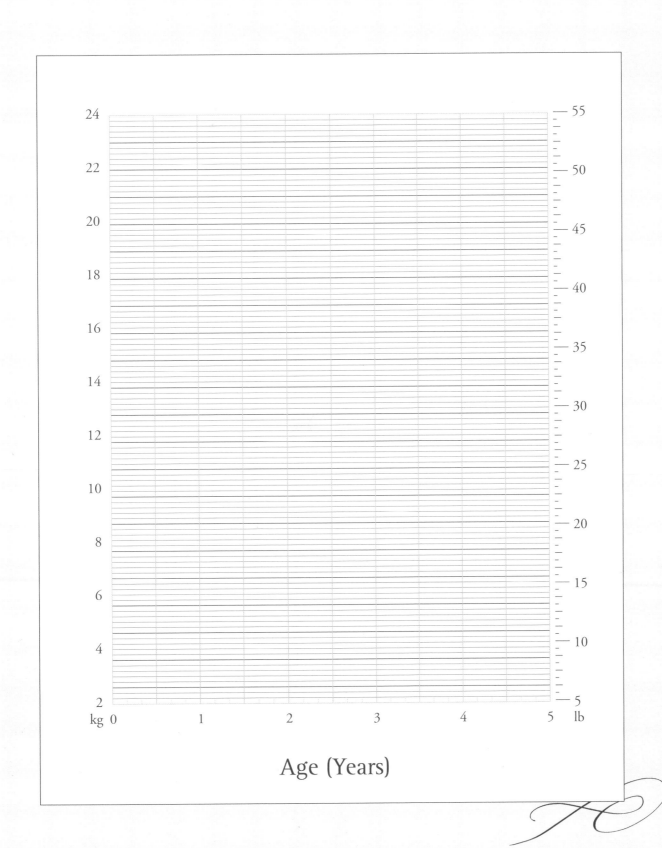

Age (Years)

71

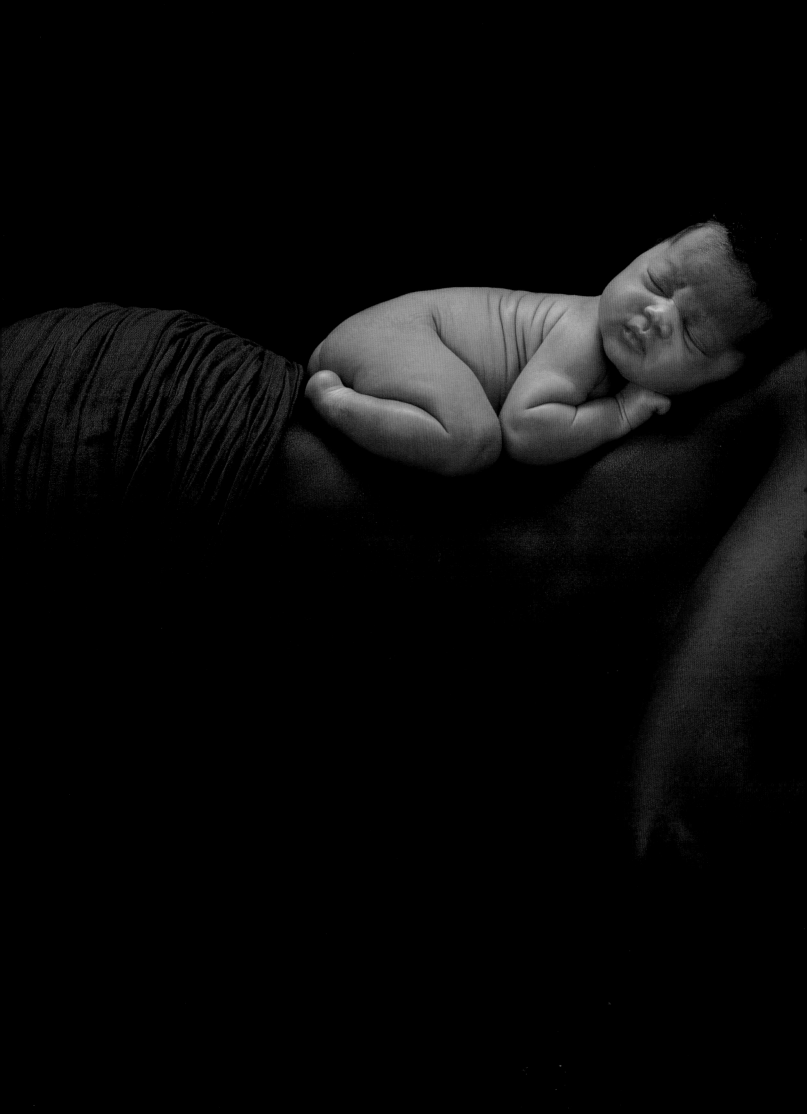

- TOOTH FAIRY'S PAGE -

I lost my first tooth on

The Tooth Fairy left me

I lost my second tooth on

The Tooth Fairy left me

- MY TEETH -

Upper Jaw Dates

8
9
16
13
24

Months

24
13
16
10
7

Lower Jaw Dates

Visits to the dentist

74

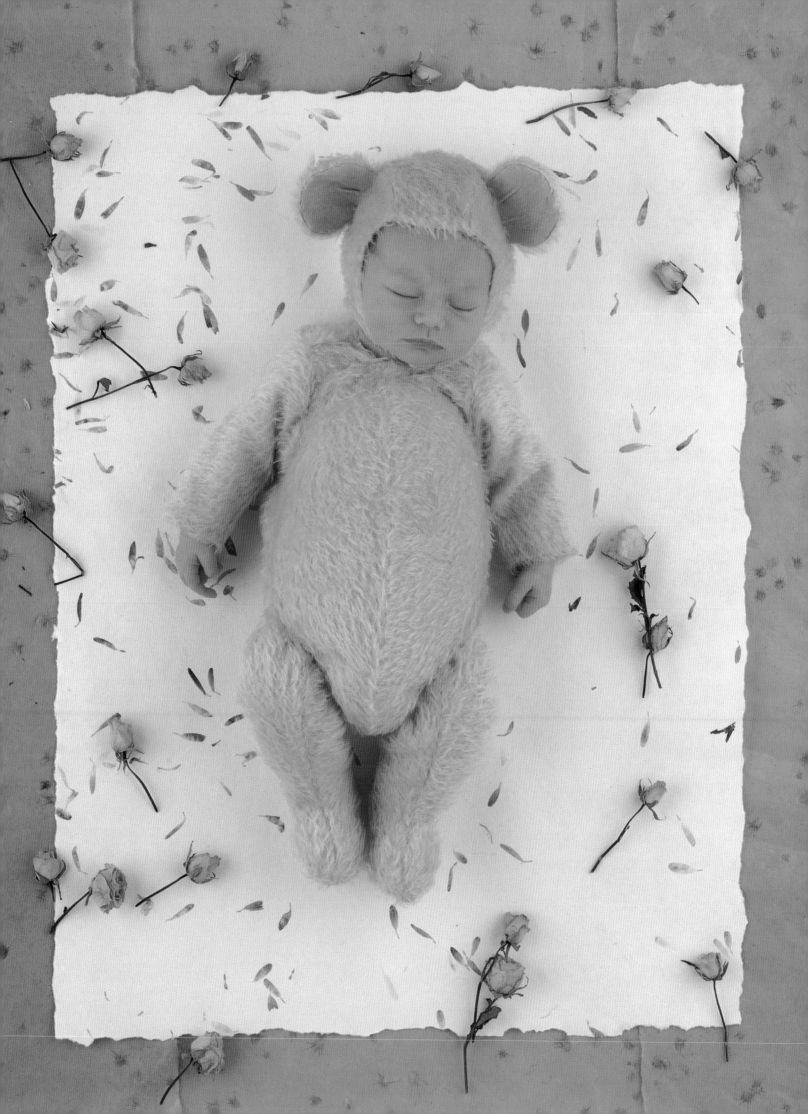

- MY HANDPRINTS -

At birth

At five years

- MY FOOTPRINTS -

At birth

At five years

- BIRTHSTONES -

JANUARY	Garnet – constancy, truth
FEBRUARY	Amethyst – sincerity, humility
MARCH	Aquamarine – courage, energy
APRIL	Diamond – innocence, success
MAY	Emerald – tranquility
JUNE	Pearl – preciousness, purity
JULY	Ruby – freedom from care, chastity
AUGUST	Moonstone – joy
SEPTEMBER	Sapphire – hope, chastity
OCTOBER	Opal – reflecting every mood
NOVEMBER	Topaz – fidelity, loyalty
DECEMBER	Turquoise – love, success

- FLOWERS -

JANUARY	Snowdrop – pure and gentle
FEBRUARY	Carnation – bold and brave
MARCH	Violet – modest
APRIL	Lily – virtuous
MAY	Hawthorn – bright and hopeful
JUNE	Rose – beautiful
JULY	Daisy – wide-eyed and innocent
AUGUST	Poppy – peaceful
SEPTEMBER	Morning Glory – easily contented
OCTOBER	Cosmos – ambitious
NOVEMBER	Chrysanthemum – cheeky and cheerful
DECEMBER	Holly – full of foresight

- STAR SIGNS -

CAPRICORN
22 December – 20 January
Resourceful, self-sufficient,
responsible

AQUARIUS
21 January – 18 February
Great caring for others, very emotional
under cool exterior

PISCES
19 February – 19 March
Imaginative, sympathetic,
tolerant

ARIES
20 March – 20 April
Brave, courageous, energetic, loyal

TAURUS
21 April – 21 May
Sensible,
loves peace and stability

GEMINI
22 May – 21 June
Unpredictable, lively,
charming, witty

CANCER
22 June – 22 July
Loves security and comfort

LEO
23 July – 23 August
Idealistic, romantic,
honorable, loyal

VIRGO
24 August – 23 September
Shy, sensitive,
values knowledge

LIBRA
24 September – 23 October
Diplomatic,
full of charm and style

SCORPIO
24 October – 22 November
Compassionate,
proud, determined

SAGITTARIUS
23 November – 21 December
Bold, impulsive,
seeks adventure

ISBN 0-7683-2082-8

© Anne Geddes 1999

www.annegeddes.com

Published in 1999 by Photogenique Publishers
(a division of Hodder Moa Beckett)
Studio 3.16, Axis Building, 1 Cleveland Road, Parnell
Auckland, New Zealand

First USA edition published in 1999
by Cedco Publishing Company
100 Pelican Way, San Rafael, CA 94901

Produced by Kel Geddes
Color separations by Image Centre
Printed by Midas Printing Limited, Hong Kong

ANNE GEDDES ™

Please write to us for a FREE FULL COLOR catalog of our fine
Anne Geddes calendars and books, Cedco Publishing Company,
100 Pelican Way, San Rafael, CA 94901
or visit our website: www.cedco.com

10 9 8 7 6 5 4 3 2 1